SPACE VOYAGE

VOYAGE
AMONG THE STARS

CATHERINE BARR

Published in 2022 by The Rosen Publishing Group, Inc.
29 East 21st Street, New York, NY 10010

Originally Published in English by Haynes Publishing under the title:
Space Pocket Manual © Catherine Barr 2019

All rights reserved. No part of this book may be reproduced in any form without permission in writing from the publisher, except by a reviewer.

Cataloging-in-Publication Data

Names: Barr, Catherine.
Title: Voyage among the stars / Catherine Barr.
Description: New York : PowerKids Press, 2022. | Series: Space voyage
Identifiers: ISBN 9781725331952 (pbk.) | ISBN 9781725331976 (library bound) | ISBN 9781725331969 (6 pack) | ISBN 9781725331983 (ebook)
Subjects: LCSH: Stars--Juvenile literature.
Classification: LCC QB801.7 B365 2022 | DDC 523.8--dc23

Design and layout by Richard Parsons

Photo Credits: Cover, p. 1 (control panel) Sky vectors/shutterstock.com; cover, p. 1 (background) sripfoto/Shutterstock.com; pp. 6-32 (background), 3, 7 (top), 8-9, 10, 13 (bottom), 16, 18, 19 (both), 20 (both), 21 (both), 22 (both), 23 (both), 24 (both), 25 (top), 27 (both); pp. 4-5, 6, 7 (bottom), 11 (top), 12, 13 (top), 14 (both), 15, 17 (both), 25 (bottom) Courtesy of NASA; p. 11 (bottom) Alamy; p. 28 (top) https://commons.wikimedia.org/wiki/File:Lipperhey_portrait.jpg; p. 28 (bottom) https://commons.wikimedia.org/wiki/File:Portrait_of_Sir_Isaac_Newton_(4670220).jpg; p. 29 (middle) https://commons.wikimedia.org/wiki/File:Portrait_of_Henry_Norris_Russell.jpg; p. 29 (bottom) https://commons.wikimedia.org/wiki/File:Launch_of_IYA_2009,_Paris_-_Grygar,_Bell_Burnell_cropped.jpg.

Manufactured in the United States of America

CPSIA Compliance Information: Batch #CSPK22. For Further Information contact Rosen Publishing, New York, New York at 1-800-237-9932.

CONTENTS

THE STARS 4
SHINING STARS 6
COLORFUL STARS 8
FOCUS ON SUPER STARS 10
STAR SYSTEMS 12
EXOPLANETS 14
SUPERNOVA! 16
ASTRONOMY 18
CONSTELLATIONS 20
THE ZODIAC 26
STARGAZERS 28
GLOSSARY 30
FOR MORE INFORMATION 31
INDEX 32

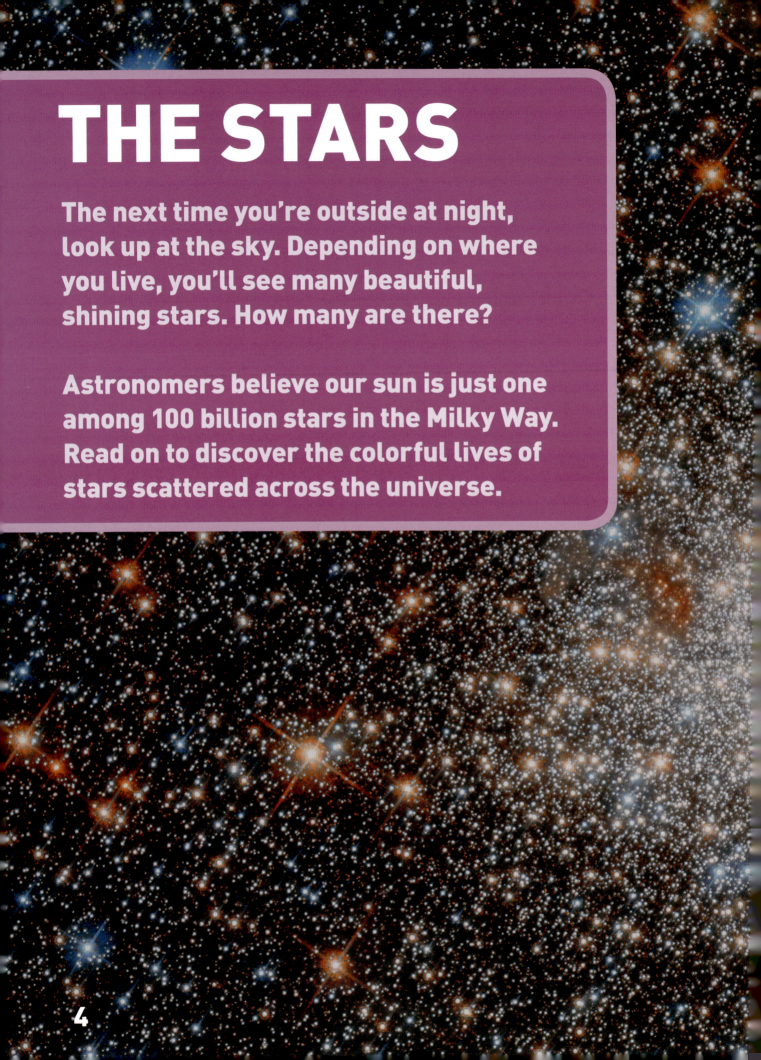

THE STARS

The next time you're outside at night, look up at the sky. Depending on where you live, you'll see many beautiful, shining stars. How many are there?

Astronomers believe our sun is just one among 100 billion stars in the Milky Way. Read on to discover the colorful lives of stars scattered across the universe.

DID YOU KNOW?

Like people, stars are born, live, and die. How long a star lives depends on a lot, but it could be millions of years!

SHINING STARS

A STAR IS BORN

In the early universe, it took 180 million years for the first stars to shine. Now there are more than 1 billion trillion stars glittering across space.

DID YOU KNOW?

Billions of stars are born each year in the whole universe of 100 billion galaxies. But the number of stars born is falling: 95 percent of all stars that will ever live have already been born!

WHY STARS SHINE

Cold clouds of the simplest gas in the universe, hydrogen, swirl into tighter and tighter balls. As gravity spins, this gas heats up. Over millions of years, as the temperature soars, a new gas called helium eventually forms. The creation of helium causes a massive explosion of energy that makes stars glow and shine with light. The sun's light energy makes all life on Earth possible.

HOW STARS DIE

Hydrogen is the fuel that keeps stars burning. When stars run out of hydrogen, they begin to die. Some blow up and explode in a spectacular final burst while others simply fade away into the mysterious blackness of the universe.

COLORFUL STARS

It might not look like it from Earth, but stars come in a rainbow of colors, depending on how hot they are. All stars are very hot, but different colors show just how hot each one is.

The H–R diagram

Astronomers plot stars according to their color and brightness. This graph shows the brightness and temperature of different stars. It is called the Hertzsprung–Russell (H–R) diagram. Most stars, like the sun, are on the main sequence with plenty of fuel to burn. When they run out of fuel, they can become cool red giants or dim white dwarfs, depending on their mass.

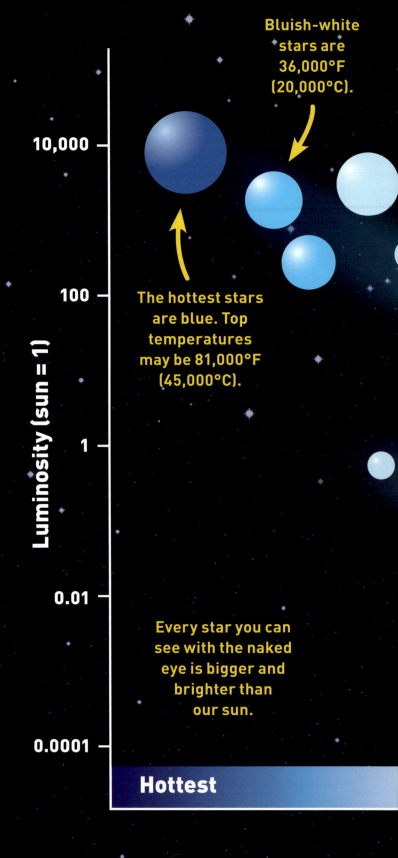

Bluish-white stars are 36,000°F (20,000°C).

The hottest stars are blue. Top temperatures may be 81,000°F (45,000°C).

Every star you can see with the naked eye is bigger and brighter than our sun.

Hottest

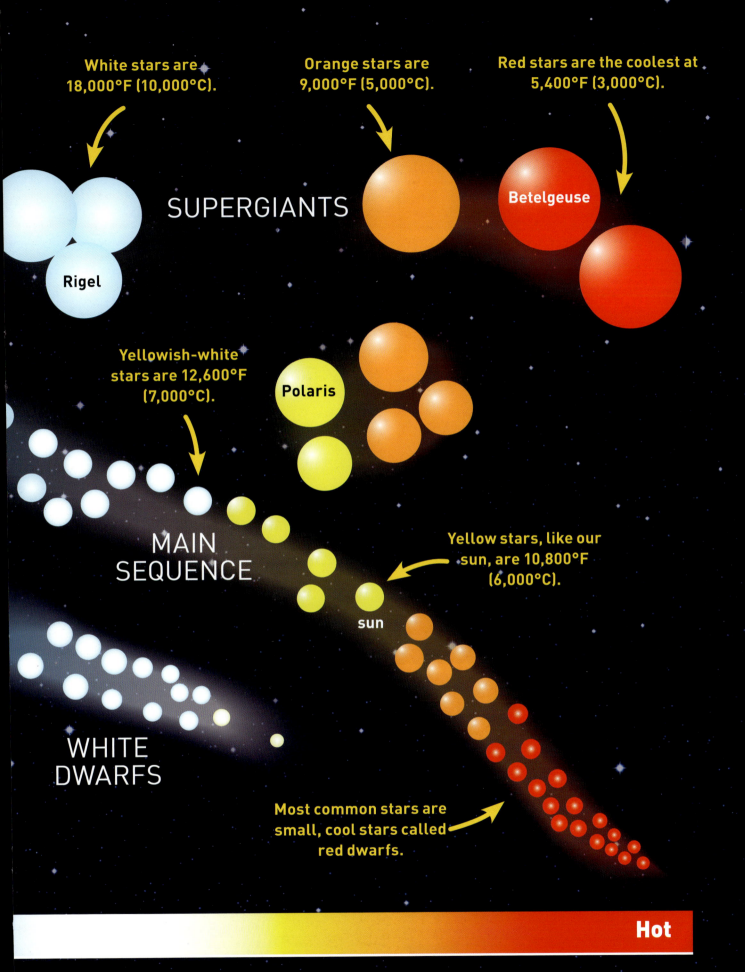

FOCUS ON SUPER STARS

THE SUN: OUR CLOSEST STAR

> This "ordinary" star provides all the energy and light that make life possible on Earth.
> The sun is our closest star, so it is the most studied star in the sky.
> It has a mysteriously superhot upper atmosphere called a corona, which glows around it.
> Supersonic solar winds flare out from the sun's surface.

DID YOU KNOW?

The sun is about halfway through its life. One day it will run out of fuel and swell up and cool down into a massive red giant. It will engulf Mercury, Venus, and probably Earth too, but not for about 5 billion years, so there's no need to worry!

BETELGEUSE: RED SUPERGIANT

- This gigantic red giant star is 10 million years old.
- It's big and burning fast. It could explode at any time as a supernova.
- It is more than 500 times bigger than the sun.
- Find it in the constellation of Orion. It is above the equator, which means that you can see it from both the Northern and Southern Hemispheres.

Betelgeuse

POLARIS: YELLOW SUPERGIANT

- This North Star is directly overhead at the North Pole.
- It's a bright supergiant that you can see from Earth.
- It is famous for guiding sailors due north while at sea.
- Find it in the constellation of Ursa Minor in the Northern Hemisphere.

Polaris, surrounded by star trails

STAR SYSTEMS

Most stars spin in pairs. These binary stars have a dimmer companion or sometimes more than one companion star. The brightness of some stars changes, and they flicker in the sky. These are called variable stars.

SIRIUS: BRIGHT BINARY STAR

- The brightest star in the sky, Sirius blazes 20 times brighter than the sun.
- It's known as the "dog star" because it's found in the constellation Canis Major, or Big Dog.
- Sirius flickers in different colors, so it is also known as the rainbow star.
- It spins with the smaller, dimmer star called Sirius B.
- It is 8.6 light-years away from Earth.

Sirius A

Sirius B
white dwarf

ALPHA CENTAURI: MULTI-STAR SYSTEM

> The nearest star to Earth, other than the sun, Alpha Centauri is "only" 4.2 light-years away.
> It is the third-brightest star in the sky.
> It is a multi-star system consisting of three stars: Alpha Centauri A, Alpha Centauri B, and Alpha Centauri C.

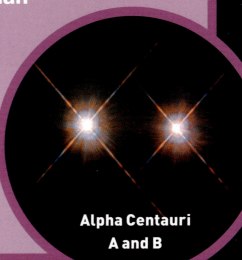

Alpha Centauri A and B

ALGOL: BLINKING DEMON STAR

> Algol is a bright triple star that looks like a binary star from Earth, but has another faint companion.
> Its brightness changes, so it is called the blinking star.
> It is about 93 light-years from Earth.
> Find it in the constellation of Perseus.

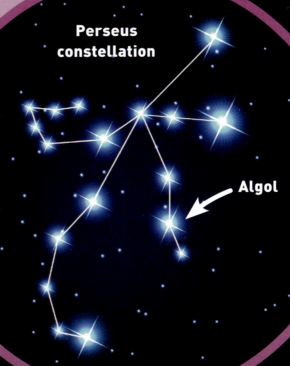

Perseus constellation

Algol

EXOPLANETS

An exoplanet is a planet orbiting a star beyond our solar system. So far, more than 4,000 exoplanets have been discovered in other galaxies. Scientists believe that every star in the universe may have an exoplanet. Some of these rocky planets are Earth-sized, while others are much bigger super-Earths.

LOOKING FOR EXOPLANETS

The Kepler Space Telescope is on the lookout for other planets in the Milky Way. So far, more than 30 have been found at the right distance from their star where liquid water is possible.

The James Webb Space Telescope is a massive new telescope that may be able to explore distant exoplanets. It will take over from the Hubble Space Telescope, which has taken some of the most amazing space photographs up until now. The James Webb Telescope will be able to make even more extraordinary discoveries possible in deep space.

The Kepler Space Telescope

4,000-PLUS EXOPLANETS

51 Pegasi was the first star found to have an orbiting planet. This first exoplanet, the size of Jupiter, was discovered in 1995. Since then, thousands more have been found in all shapes and sizes. They are common in our galaxy and new discoveries are made each year.

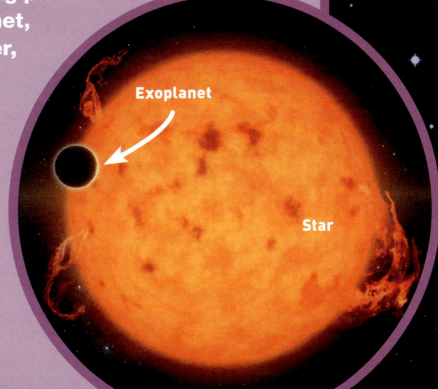

Exoplanet

Star

DID YOU KNOW?

Scientists think there could be billions of Earth-size planets within the Milky Way galaxy alone. One of the problems is that exoplanets are difficult to see, even with telescopes, as they are hidden by the brightness of the stars that they orbit.

SUPERNOVA!

A supernova is the massive explosion of a dying star. Supernovae can outshine whole galaxies and give out more energy than our sun will in its entire lifetime. These events create all the heavy metals, such as iron and gold, that exist in the universe.

HOW LONG DOES IT TAKE?

Stars take a few million years to die, then in less than a second, a star can collapse, sending out massive galactic shockwaves. It brightens in a few months and then takes years to fade away. One of the most famous leftover supernovae is the Crab Nebula (or M1), which is 10 light-years across. It was first spotted by Chinese astronomers in 1054 and has been observed by astronomers ever since. The star is still dying, so the supernova is still growing.

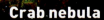
Crab nebula

MAKING ATOMS

The first atoms were made 380,000 years after the Big Bang, the moment when the universe formed. These atoms and every atom ever since were made in the stars. As the stars die, they explode in a burst of gas and dust. This dust and gas thrown out into space forms all the matter that exists in the universe.

GOLD DUST

When really big stars explode and die or when two stars crash, they make heavy metals such as gold. Gold dust is then hurled out across the universe. About 3.9 billion years ago, Earth was bombarded by meteorites full of gold. This gold sank down into the center of the planet.

ASTRONOMY

Astronomy is the study of the cosmos: the planets, stars, asteroids, comets, and the galaxies in space. From studying stars to understanding space to teaching and inventing, there are lots of ways to be an astronomer if you are star crazy!

STAR MAPPING

As long ago as 1000 BCE, the Babylonians were mapping the sky. Greeks, Romans, and many others joined these sparkly dots to draw familiar patterns of stars in the night sky. This helped astronomers find particular stars or galaxies and learn about the cosmos. It also helped them track time, which was useful for farming and getting around.

FINDING THE WAY

Early humans probably stared at the stars to track their path. The bright North Star, Polaris, points north, and familiar patterns of other stars helped travelers and sailors map their way across land and sea.

Polaris, the North Star

TAKE A LOOK

Today, everyone from space scientists to schoolchildren can explore the skies in different ways. From using giant telescopes in observatories to mobile phone apps in your yard, people on Earth are looking up and learning about their place in space.

CONSTELLATIONS

Astronomers have divided the sky up into 88 areas, or constellations. Within each constellation there is a named group of stars, which look from Earth as if they make up shapes in the sky. This makes them easy to recognize and study. In fact, stars are randomly dotted in space.

The Orion constellation

DID YOU KNOW?

You see different constellations depending on whether you are stargazing in the Southern or the Northern Hemisphere.

Orion: the Hunter

Find Orion's belt of three bright stars in the middle of the constellation, and the star Betelgeuse in his armpit. It can be seen from both hemispheres.

Canis Major: the Big Dog

This constellation can be seen in both hemispheres at different times. It contains Sirius, or the dog star. Sirius is one of the closest stars to Earth.

Sirius

Ursa Major: the Big Dipper

The Big Dipper, also known as the Plough, is a really easy constellation to spot. You can find it in summer in the northernmost part of the sky.

Ursa Minor: the Little Dipper

Ursa is Latin for "bear," and this is the little one. Spot the North Star, Polaris, shining at the tip of this constellation, which lies in the northern sky.

Pegasus: the Winged Horse

This constellation is famous for hosting the first exoplanet (planet outside the solar system) found around a normal star.

Draco: the Dragon

Seen in the Northern Hemisphere, this is one of the largest constellations. It snakes its way across the sky like a serpent, or dragon.

Hercules: the Hero

The figure is usually drawn with his foot on the head of Draco, which is appropriate as one of the labors of the mythical hero Hercules was to slay a dragon.

Cygnus: the Swan

Cygnus is large and easy to spot. The Milky Way passes through the middle of the cross, littering it with the richest star fields in the northern sky.

TWINKLE TWINKLE

If you look hard on a clear night, you might see 2,000 stars scattered across the night sky. These stars appear to twinkle, although in fact this isn't the case. It is only viewing them through Earth's atmosphere that makes them sparkle.

ANCIENT LIGHT

Light from stars takes a long time to reach Earth. Some stars we can see are already dead. We can still see them because their light has taken so long to reach us. The visible energy waves travel at the speed of light, 186,000 miles (300,000 km) per second! The star designated as HD 140283 is currently the oldest known star in the galaxy. It is called the Methuselah star after a story in the Bible of a man who lived for 969 years.

Methuselah star

THE ZODIAC

The zodiac is an area of sky that maps the sun's path over a year. In the zodiac, there are 12 groups of stars. Some people believe that there is a link between these groups of stars and people's lives on Earth, which is called astrology. Unlike astronomy, astrology is not a science.

- Capricornus "Sea Goat" — December 22 – January 19
- Aquarius "Water Bearer" — January 20 – February 18
- Pisces "Fishes" — February 19 – March 20
- Aries "Ram" — March 21 – April 19
- Taurus "Bull" — April 20 – May 20
- Gemini "The Twins" — May 21 – June 20
- Cancer "Crab" — June 21 – July 22
- Leo "Lion" — July 23 – August 22
- Virgo "Virgin" — August 23 – September 22
- Libra "Scales" — September 23 – October 22
- Scorpius "Scorpion" — October 23 – November 21
- Sagittarius "Archer" — November 22 – December 21
- Ophiuchus "Snake Bearer" — Not used in astrology

WHO FOUND THEM?

The zodiac constellations were found by the Babylonians, who passed their knowledge on to the ancient Greeks, who then told the Romans, and now we recognize these constellations in the sky.

Leo, the "Lion," is one of the few zodiac constellations that looks like its name. Gemini, the "Twins," looks like two stick figures with arms touching.

Leo the Lion

STARGAZERS

HANS LIPPERSHEY

(1570–1619)
This glasses maker from the Netherlands invented the lens that made it possible to see things that were far away as if they were close up. It is likely that he invented the telescope that Galileo later improved.

ISAAC NEWTON

(1642–1727)
He was an Englishman who discovered the laws of gravity. The sun's gravity pulls Earth and all the other planets around it. Without the pull of gravity, we would drift off into space. Newton also invented the type of telescope that is widely used today to look up at the stars.

EJNAR HERTZSPRUNG

(1873–1967)
This Danish astronomer was famous for working out how the brightness of a star related to its color.

HENRY RUSSELL

(1877–1957)
This American astrophysicist was interested in how stars evolved. With Hertzsprung, he created the famous H–R diagram that maps the stars according to brightness and temperature.

DAME JOCELYN BELL BURNELL

(1943–)
She is a British scientist from Northern Ireland who discovered a new kind of star. She found stars whose light changed between strong and weak light, or "pulsed." These stars are called pulsars.

GLOSSARY

astronomer a scientist who studies space
atmosphere the mixture of gases that surround a planet
collapse to fall down or cave in
constellation a group of stars that forms a certain shape in the sky and has been given a name
galaxy a large group of stars, planets, gas, and dust that form a unit within the universe
gravity the force that pulls objects toward the center of a planet or star
hemisphere one half of Earth
light-year the distance light can travel in one year
solar system the sun and all the space objects that orbit it, including the planets and their moons
telescope a tool that makes faraway objects look bigger and closer
universe everything that exists

FOR MORE INFORMATION

BOOKS

Beer, Julie, and Stephanie Warren Drimmer. *Can't Get Enough Space Stuff*. Washington, DC: National Geographic, 2022.

Nargi, Lela. *Mysteries of Planets, Stars, and Galaxies*. North Mankato, MN: Capstone Press, 2021.

WEBSITES

www.ducksters.com/science/physics/space_exploration_timeline.php
Use this timeline to mark when different parts of the solar system were discovered and explored.

kids.nationalgeographic.com/space/article/milky-way
Learn more about the Milky Way here.

spaceplace.nasa.gov/search/stars/
Check out NASA's website for kids that tells all about stars.

Publisher's note to educators and parents: Our editors have carefully reviewed these websites to ensure that they are suitable for students. Many websites change frequently, however, and we cannot guarantee that a site's future contents will continue to meet our high standards of quality and educational value. Be advised that students should be closely supervised whenever they access the internet.

INDEX

Algol 13
Alpha Centauri 13
astrology 26
Betelgeuse 11, 21
Big Bang 17
Burnell, Jocelyn Bell 29
constellations 11, 12, 13, 20, 21, 22, 23, 24, 26
Crab Nebula 16
Earth 7, 8, 10, 11, 12, 13, 14, 15, 17, 19, 20, 21, 25, 26, 28
Hertzsprung, Ejnar 29
Hertzsprung–Russell (H–R) diagram 8, 29
Hubble Space Telescope 14
James Webb Space Telescope 14
Kepler Space Telescope 14
Lippershey, Hans 28
main sequence 8
Methuselah star 25
Milky Way 4, 14, 15, 24
Newton, Isaac 28
Polaris 11, 19, 22
pulsars 29
red giants 8, 10
Russell, Henry 29
Sirius 12, 21
speed of light 25
sun 4, 7, 8, 10, 11, 12, 13, 16, 26, 28
supergiant 11
supernova 11, 16